TIME TO GROW UP

The Danger of
Being a Baby Christian

BETTY MILES

WESTBOW
PRESS®
A DIVISION OF THOMAS NELSON
& ZONDERVAN

WestBow Press books may be ordered through booksellers or by contacting:

WestBow Press
A Division of Thomas Nelson & Zondervan
1663 Liberty Drive
Bloomington, IN 47403
www.westbowpress.com
844-714-3454

ISBN: 978-1-6642-3965-4 (sc)
ISBN: 978-1-6642-3964-7 (e)

Print information available on the last page.

WestBow Press rev. date: 09/16/2021

CONTENTS

I dedicate this book to anyone who has gone through the trauma of sexual abuse, and all the "tag alongs" that come along with it… like verbal and physical abuse (especially if you knew not to tell…so you didn't).

There is only one answer, or Person, who can give us back our self-esteem and a new perception of who we really are. What a discovery!

I want to thank my daughter (in-law), Betty Lorenz, who helped me get through this project! She was always there to proof read, type, and most importantly…to encourage!

*All profits from this book will go to prison ministry

NOTES IN CONTEXT

Page 88 in this book is Robert Morris' paraphrase of what John said about his baptism in his book, "The God I Never Knew" (page 90 in Morris' book). Published by WaterBrook, a division of Crown Publishing.

Page 53 in this book is a quote from Oswald Chambers from his book, "My Utmost For His Highest" (page 24 in his book). Published in 1935, Renewed in 1963 by Oswald Chambers to Discovery House Publishers.

THE WOMAN AT THE WELL

Psalms 103: 10,11 NKJ

"He has not dealt with us according to our sins, nor punished us according to our iniquities. For as the heavens are high above the earth, so great is His mercy toward those who fear Him."

*All other scriptures in Chapter 1 are from John 4 The Living Bible

The Woman at the Well

S amaria was an area that was carefully avoided by most Jews. Jesus, however, was not one of them. He and his disciples were leaving Judea and returning to the province of Galilee. But instead of going out of their way to avoid Samaria, they chose to go through this town.

After walking most of the morning Jesus was tired and thirsty and ready for a cool drink of water from Jacob's well, which was not far from the small village of Sychar. The disciples had gone into Sychar to purchase some food.

John 4:4 (TLB) tells us "He has to go through Samaria on the way." I think it was not geography he was concerned about!

But rather that He was aware that He was going to meet someone who needed some direction in her life - so He had to go through Samaria.

When He arrived at the well, no one was there. Most people came to water their animals at the cooler part of the day - morning or evening.

He saw her coming. I'm sure He thought, "This is the one for whom I'm come."

When the woman arrived she too was weary. It was a good five mile walk from Samaria to the well. When she saw the Jewish man sitting at the well, she ignored Him. She was shocked when He asked her for a drink. She turned and looked at Him.

Then she decided to let him know what she was thinking! "How is it that a Jew would ask a despised Samaritan for anything - usually they never speak to us!"(John 4:7-9 TLB) Jesus replied, "If you only knew what a wonderful gift God has for you, and who I am, you would ask me for living water!" (John 4:10 TLB)

I imagine her as she was looking at him, with her hands on her hips, and a smile on her face, and said, "But you don't even have a rope or a bucket, and this is a very deep well. Where would you get this living water?" (John 4:11 TLB) Jesus stood up, and walked toward the woman. He said to her, "People soon become thirsty again after drinking this water. But the water I give them becomes a perpetual spring within them forever with eternal life." (John 4:13,14 TLB)

She paused for a moment and thought to herself, "Where have I heard that before?" It reminded her of the conversations she had heard from her people when she was a child. "There is One coming who will be called the Messiah! He would give them living water and eternal life." She knew there was something different about this man... she could "feel" it even as He spoke!

She wanted to hear more. "Please sir, give me some of this water! Then I'll never be thirsty again and have to make this long trip out here everyday." (John 4:15 TLB)

He gently touched her shoulder and said, "Go and get your husband." (John 4:16 TLB) Almost as soon as He touched her, she knew immediately this was not the touch of an ordinary man! She knew that touch well!

The touch of most men always meant they wanted something from her. This was a very different touch, she knew in that moment that God was real! She looked into His eyes, and softly spoke, "But I'm not married." (John 4:17 TLB)

"All too true!" Jesus replied, "For you have had five husbands, and you aren't even married to the man you're living with now." (John 4:12, 18 TLB) She looked at him, still shocked that He knew who she was and knew her history with men. She was convinced if He was not the Messiah, He certainly was a prophet. Yet, when He touched her, she felt a presence she had never felt before. Something in the very depths of her being had sprung up within her at that first touch. She finally answered Him. "Well, I know the Messiah will come - the One they call the Christ - and when He comes, He will explain everything to us." (John 4:25 TLB)

Then Jesus told her, "I am the Messiah!" (John 4:26 TLB)

Just at that moment the disciples arrived. They were surprised to find Jesus talking to the woman, but none of them asked why, or what they were discussing. (John 4:27 TLB) She turned and looked at them - then she left her water pot beside the well and hurried to the village and told everyone, "Come and meet a man who told me all the things I ever did! Can this be the Messiah?" So the people came streaming from the village to see him! (John 4:28-30 TLB)

Her countenance had changed! The people who knew her couldn't believe it was the same woman - she looked different!

Those who usually would have avoided her, ran beside her as she told of the man at the well. Many from the village believed he was the Messiah because of the woman's report, "He told me everything I ever did." (John 4:39 TLB)

When they came out to see him at the well, they begged him to stay at their village. And he did stay, for two days. Long enough for many of them to believe in Him after hearing Him. "Now we believe in Him because we have heard him ourselves, not just because of what you told us." (John 4:40-43 TLB)

It was evident that day that the Samaritans as well as the Jews could be saved, and proof as well, that no matter her former life, the woman at the well was changed forever. This woman discovered what Jesus talked about in John (7:37-38 TLB) "…Anyone who is thirsty may come to me! Anyone who believes in me may come and drink! For the Scriptures declare, 'Rivers of living water will flow from his heart.'" I, along with the woman at the well, have found this to be a very true statement!

2

FIVE HUSBANDS

1st Peter 2:9b NKJ

"…you are priests of the King, you are holy and pure, you are God's very own. All this so that you may show to others how God called you of darkness into His wonderful light."

YES!!!

W hen reading this story, I'm drawn to the fact that this woman had five husbands! Certainly this is enough on which to to build a reputation, but not much on which to build a life! I'm sure many reading this will say, "I've had more than one husband, and God has still loved and forgiven me." Others can add even greater numbers - but few, I believe would want to admit to five! Let me assure you, that this is not an easy thing to admit.

But it's true. I've had five husbands, and no explanation will every convince me how this happened. I've alluded to it I suppose, but no one has ever heard one say it! So much shame goes with the words! It sounds a little better to add, I've only had three that ended in divorce! Way too many, either way!

But all five are deceased, and in case you are wondering…the each died of natural causes. Before I tell you my story, I have to say that God has blessed me so in spite of my mistakes (that word isn't strong enough), but His forgiveness knows no bounds!

I read this recently: "One can be wounded in childhood and never mature emotionally as an adult." I know for certain that is not an overstatement. I have only a few memories of outstanding events in my younger years - but the ones that have haunted me throughout my life have never left me!

I had secrets I could tell no one. What does a child do when she (or he) can't share their painful secrets? In my case, I pretended that everything was okay. I may have convinced everyone around me, but I never bought the lie!

I was molested on two occasions when I was a little girl. The first time was when we lived in Tecumseh. I was probably in the first grade at Bernard School.

I remember his name well, but I won't say it (This was well over eighty years ago!) He was the grade school principal. For some reason he was sitting in for our classroom teacher who was somewhere else. All the students were at their desks. He called me by name and told me to come up to his desk. He sat me on his lap while he was looking (or talking) to the other students. I know this doesn't sound reasonable, but he was molesting me with his left hand at the time! I remember I was afraid and didn't know what to do. I just remember him finally taking me from his lap and telling me to go back to my desk. Remember, this was the principal!

I think it was the next day when he was on playground duty, and he had his back to me. I walked around in front of him and looked into his eyes. He quickly looked down at me and turned, hurriedly, to the other side of the playground.

I told no one what had happened. For some reason, I knew it must have been my fault. At least I knew I wasn't supposed to tell anyone! And I didn't. My first secret - and it haunted me.

A few years later, our family went to on our first vacation to see my daddy's family, his sister, her husband and their children who lived in Texas. When it was time to leave, a few days later, my aunt wanted me to stay with them. Daddy finally said "yes", but told me it might be several weeks before they could come back and get me.

By that time war was imminent, every time a plane would fly over, I was scared and wanted to go home. But I had to stay until Daddy could come. My older cousin, Billy, wanted me to go with him across the road from their house, into the heavy trees, so he could show me something. Of course I was excited to see what he was talking about. When we were deep into the woods, he suddenly squatted down on the ground and pulled me to him. He was raping me and I began to scream. I looked through the trees and could see my cousin W.G. walking down the road. I'm sure he could see her as well. I screamed her name louder, and he let me go.

I was straightening my clothes and running as fast as I could. I finally caught up with her, and we kept walking. She said nothing - I said nothing. I always wondered if she knew what was happening. I'm sure she heard me screaming. Still - we just kept waking…saying nothing!

Somehow there was an inner voice that told me, "This is all your fault again - you are a bad person." Of course now I know this is the voice of the enemy! If he can convince you of this lie, you can be forever bound! I was.

I didn't realize it at the time, but my moral compass had been shattered. I was an enabler. I allowed men to abuse me!

Of my five marriages, only one God arranged - the other four just happened!

3

THE GOOD HUSBAND (THERE WAS ONE!)

Romans 8:28 NKJ

"And we know that all things work together for good to those who love God, to those who are called according to His purpose."

(Romans 8:28 is such an amazing scripture that illustrates for me - how even when I didn't have a clue, God knew I had a purpose!)

Marriage number three was the only marriage that I had that was not a disaster. Jack Lorenz was the high school principal at Okeene.

I was teaching in a small school near Oklahoma City, when he was there to see his friend who was also the principal. I had stopped by his office for some reason, and he introduced me to Jack.

It wasn't long before Jack called me and asked me if he could take me out to dinner. Of course (as was my habit) I said "yes".

He seemed like a good person, and he was. To be honest, God actually set this one up for me! I didn't know it at the time, but just a year or two ago, God revealed that to me when I was in my "quiet time".

God knew something about Jack that neither of us knew. He knew Jack had cancer. He also knew that Jack was not a Christian - he had heard his mother's prayers, and He knew I knew how to lead someone to the Lord. He also knew Jack didn't have long to live.

After several months of dating, he asked me to marry him. He was the kindest man I had ever known. Of course, I said "yes".

I had gotten pregnant on our honeymoon, and Jack was so excited, because he so wanted a son! He was working at school, but it was getting more difficult as there was little they could do for his pain. He had been sent to several doctors, but apparently in the fifties, stomach cancer was hard to diagnose.

The day finally came when his doctor sent him to an

15

Enid hospital for exploratory surgery. His doctor gave me little hope.

The evening before the surgery, we were lying in bed, and I sat up and touched his shoulder and said, "Jack, there is only one way I can handle this, that is if I know for certain you will accept Jesus as your Lord and Saviour." He turned and looked at me and said, "Yes, I will. I don't know why I've waited so long!"

The surgery was too late - the cancer had spread too far. They sent him back to the hospital at Okeene. He never came home.

One day they called me to come quickly to the hospital. When I walked into the room, he was lying on a movable gurney! I saw his spirit leave his body! It went straight up!

4

THE PROMISE

John 8:32 TLB

"...and you shall know the truth, and the truth shall make you free."

---

t was several years after Jack died that I decided to go to the University of Oklahoma and get my doctorate. I had already completed my masters at Central State University when I was eight months pregnant with Jack Todd. Why I made this decision, I'll never know. It just seemed like the right thing to do at the time.

I was accepted at OU, and hired to teach in the fall as an associate in the speech department, while I worked on my degree.

Vanessa, my daughter from my first marriage, was not happy about moving from Okeene. She was fifteen at the time, and I can look back now and realize I should have considered her first - but I seldom looked at what was best for all of us! "Too late smart," I always said.

I bought a house and we made the move. I really didn't know what lay ahead. At the end of summer, I was among those accepted into the doctorate program. When it was time for the fall semester, I realized I was not prepared for the pressure!

I had gotten used to someone being "in charge." I still missed the someone one who really cared about me - and he was gone. Even though I knew where he was, I still grieved.

When school started in the fall I realized, that first day, that I was a basket case. When the hour was over, I went to the head of the department and resigned! Of course, I still needed a job! I called the superintendent of schools in Norman, and he had an opening at a middle school and I was hired!

This was my routine: I taught all day, got in my car and cried all the way home. The next morning I cried all the way to school. I did my job and kept this up until I realized I needed professional help.

As I recall, someone recommended this very expensive psychiatrist, who handed me a tissue every so often to dry my tears. I don't recall he talked much - nor I think, even listened. I decided there had to be a better way…

I know Vanessa and Jack must have had a hard time watching all of this. My sister, Georgia, came and stayed with us as often as she could. My daddy came from Florida, but I think God just allowed time to heal me. He knew He had a purpose for my life and kept me sane!

Believe it or not, I was rehired back at my school in Norman! But Vanessa still wanted to go back to Okeene.

I followed my usual routine, and called Mr Dixon to see if he had a vacancy. He did! It was a second and third grad combination - but it was Okeene!

I wish I could say I had finally found peace in my life, but that didn't happen until I was past fifty years old.

Actually, I wasn't looking for "someone to take me away from all this," because I loved teaching and soon I was back in high school with my favorite age group. Now my daughter was a senior, and my son in grade school. A friend from another city called me and asked me if I would do her a favor. She said she had a boyfriend she was wanting to get rid of, and would I let her introduce him to me - because, maybe I would like him!

Well, of course I would! What are friends for? As usual, this was a man who needed fixing!

My sister reminded me later, when we were dating,

we came to Oklahoma City to see her. When Georgia and I were alone, I told her, "I've got to get rid of this guy!" The next time I talked to her, I told her we were getting married!

I won't go far into those years, they were such a mess! He certainly needed fixing - and I couldn't even fix myself. Thank God, I later learned none of us can fix ourselves! I taught school at this small town close to Enid. That year I actually was awarded the Teacher of the Year award in Garfield county! Our little school had won 1st place in the state - One Act Plan contest in our class! I credited the teacher's award to that achievement!

Finally, in this marriage, we actually went to our pastor for counseling. After a brief period of time, he said we needed professional help, and he sent us to a private institution in Dallas, Tx. We both were interviewed, given tests and the next day came back in for the results. The doctor told me I needed counseling and suggested I stay for a few days - or as long as needed. When my husband left, the doctor told me he had "thrown" the test, and answered everything as if he were 100% perfect! He knew he didn't want help.

I finally realized I was in a mental hospital!

I was in "lock down!" I knew I was sane - troubled - but sane. Each little room had locks on the door. I could use no phone, had no purse - nothing. There was a hole in each door where you could look out! I could see eyes looking my way! I truly was in a cracker box! There had been a movie recently by that name, and now I knew how it felt to be caged!

Back home my husband called my parents in Florida, my sister, my boss, and everyone else I knew and told them

I was in a mental institution. Of course I could call no one! (Later, they all told me they knew I wasn't crazy!)

I found a book someone had left there, and I can't remember if this was the title of the book, or the main thesis, called "You can't put God in a box." It helped get me through those first few days.

When I finally got home, things were no better and I gave my husband a choice, "you either go back to Dallas, and retake that test or I am leaving!" To my surprise, he went back to Dallas.

I went back to work the next day after I got home. I can't remember how long he stayed in Dallas, I just remember the doctor called me to say, "Your husband just checked himself out of our facility and I felt I should call you to tell you that you should not be there when he arrives. I think your life is in danger."

My stepson helped me load up my car and my son and I drove to Enid. I rented the first apartment that was available. Later, I bought a home in a small addition close to my school. Before the new school year began, Mr. Dixon called me to tell me he had a vacancy! "Could I come back to Okeene?" Of course I could!

Some may be thinking, what's going on between Mr Dixon and this speech teacher? I think I should "put to rest" those questions, but as I write this, I can see how one might wonder!

I was having "Sunday dinner" with friends and Mildred asked me, "Betty, did you know there are rumors that you are having an affair with Mr. Dixon?" I couldn't believe it, and assured her it wasn't true! I was troubled all weekend, and could hardly wait until Monday morning to speak with Mr. Dixon.

As I walked into the building, Mr Dixon was standing, greeting everyone who came in! I asked him if I could speak with him. He could see I was serious, and I told him the gossip I had heard. He gave me this advise, "Don't address it. You and I both know this is untrue. Ignore it." So this is what I did.

One Sunday, years later, this subject - gossip - was addressed in our Sunday school lesson which I taught. Mr Dixon's wife, Rosemary, was in my class! I asked her if she had heard the rumor. She shook her head "yes." I assured her it never happened and thought this was good advice of how we should respond to gossip! If it's untrue, ignore it! And move on!

SEARCHING FOR ANSWERS

Philippians 1:6 NKJ

"Being confident of this very thing - That He who has begun a good work in you will complete it until the day of Jesus Christ.

This is a promise you can take to the bank! I know from experience…God means what He says! Hang in there!!

I grew up in church! At least, I don't remember the early years when we didn't go to church.

My Grandpa Woods (my mother's father) owned the packing plant in Holdenville, Oklahoma, where we lived. And being a butcher himself, taught my dad, George, all the skills a good butcher would ever need to know, and he excelled.

When my sister and I were in grade school, and my brother was a baby, we moved to Tecumseh, Oklahoma, where Daddy had gotten a job at the packing plant. In recent years I began to wonder why we made that move, and then I realized that God had a part in that decision.

God knew that the Baptist pastor, Dr S.S. Stover, made frequent trips to the packing plant to visit the workers who had rather unpleasant conditions in which to work. My Dad caught his eye. They got acquainted, and Brother Stover continued his visits.

It wasn't long before we were attending church at the First Baptist Church. Brother Stover continued witnessing to my dad, and he soon made the decision to accept Jesus as his Saviour. Not long after that he realized God had called him to preach! Brother Stover not only led him to the Lord, he mentored him for a year!

My father had a fifth grade education and he and Brother Stover were life long friends. Later, he and Mrs. Stover left Tecumseh to go to Brazil as Missionaries. Even then, they kept in touch.

There was no question God had called my father to

preach! One of the things I noticed as a child was the skills he had as a butcher.

Remember, in those days, when a farmer or rancher was ready to butcher an animal, it drew a crowd. Living in the country, my Daddy was the main attraction! I watched once, how quickly and skillfully he moved the sharp knife and removed the skin - then continued until the job was finished and the meat was ready to be sent to the kitchen!

God used these skills to give him an opportunity to reach out to the men who he could later tell about Jesus! And he did!

Daddy had lost his mother when he was in grade school. It wasn't long before his dad brought another woman, and her boys into their home.

My daddy, George, was watching one day when one of her boys kicked his dog. That was all he needed. He threw the boy to the ground, and the boy started screaming! At that moment his mother looked out to see what was happening, and she immediately called for my grandpa to come out and take care of George! And he did. He told George to go pack his clothes while he hitched his horses up to the wagon.

It was his sister who told me this. Daddy never talked about how he was raised. What happened next was sad to hear. He took George into town and left him at the local feed store and told him he was on his own.

And he was….

Mother, on the other hand, came from a completely different kind of family. Grandpa Woods had a butcher shop in Lawrenceville, Illinois. They lived in a big two story home. I always loved to hear Mother's stories about her childhood. She was spoiled, and the pet of the neighborhood.

I mention this to say how their upbringing was so completely opposite - except neither was raised going to church.

Mother always said she didn't think she was called to be a preacher's wife, but I always felt she was. Daddy was such a good preacher, and was always loved by his "flock."

I can remember when Daddy was preaching, and if he used incorrect grammar, Mother always took notes, and would later show him the correct usage. Daddy was always a quick learner and I never heard him complain about her correcting him. God knew what He was doing when He brought them together.

When my sister was nine years old, she went "forward" during the invitation at church and accepted Jesus as her Saviour - since I always did what she did, I followed her down the aisle. We were both both baptized.

When I was twelve years old, I realized I hadn't understood what I was doing when I followed her, but since I was a member of the church, I didn't want anyone to know. But one thing I did know, is that if I died, I would not go to heaven. I lived with this fear until I was sixteen years old, and our youth group went to Falls Creek, a youth camp near Davis, Oklahoma - where hundreds, now thousands of young people go during the summer months. They hear the best evangelists and musicians around! There is always a sweet, sweet spirit in that place!

They had just issued an invitation while we were all standing. I remember clearly when a woman behind me, tapped me on the shoulder and whispered in my ear, "Don't you think you should go to the alter?" I was so happy that God had told that woman what I needed! What a relief! Talk about a burden lifted! I was so excited that I no longer had to carry that burden. I can still remember the joy I had as our group left the tabernacle that evening! It was wonderful!

My Dad baptized me soon after that and I can remember thinking that being baptized "completed" my salvation!

I went off to college in the fall that year and got caught up with what was always first in my life when I was in high school - speech, drama, plays and the theater.

I joined "College Players" at Oklahoma Baptist University and had something to do with every play we produced. Either I was acting, or behind the scenes. It was what was first in my life! It's hard to admit this, but I didn't really understand I had a problem.

I was always ready to compete in every area in both high school and college - and yes, I wanted to prove that I was a good person.

That continued as I began my teaching career. I loved teaching. Even as a child, playing with my sister, I always wanted to be be the teacher! I later received "Teacher of the Year Awards" in two different counties! Wasn't this proof that I was ok? But it was never enough. I still had little self worth outside of school!

I didn't realize it, but I was driven by what happened to me as a little girl! My goal in life (not knowingly) was to prove I really was a good person! I may have convinced some, but never myself!

Yes, something was missing, and I was so ignorant of what it was!

DADDY WAS A PREACHER

Romans 11:29 NKJ

"For the gifts and the calling of God are irrevocable."

Daddy's first church, when he began to preach, was in Winfield, Kansas. The one thing I've never forgotten was what happened after the last service there. My sister her had all kinds of allergies, and the doctor had advised us to move back to Oklahoma. She was allergic to everything in that area!

I'll never for get what happened when daddy told them we were going to have to move. After the service, we all went outside the church. The small crowd of people encircled our family as they sang "When we all get to heaven, what rejoicing that will be!" Many were crying as they sang! It certainly touched my heart.

He next pastored a church in Cushing, Oklahoma. I remember the little house we lived in. As I recall, the neighbor next door invited my sister and me into her house. While the woman was out of the room, I spotted a quarter under my chair and I picked it up and I put it in my shoe! We didn't stay long and went directly home. I took the quarter out of my shoe and showed it to Daddy! I said, "Look what I found outside!" Daddy said, "This sure feels warm to have been outside!" I answered, "Yes, but I put it in my shoe when I found it." That satisfied Daddy, but I felt awful, for not only stealing, but also for lying! It was a hard lesson, but I learned that nothing you ever steal, or lie about is worth the internal pain you will suffer!

Later we moved to a rural church called "Rock Creek," close to Shawnee, Oklahoma.

I remember there was a black church a mile or two from our church. Daddy and the pastor were friends. One day they decided our church would walk over to their church after Sunday school. I can still remember that little crowd walking that dusty road, going inside and worshipping together.

Once Daddy preached in his church and he also preached in ours! I never knew anything about racial prejudice in those days.

I remember one time when I was staying with my grandma in Oklahoma City, there was a drugstore called Katz. Grandma had given me money to go to the soda fountain while she shopped. I noticed they had two soda fountains! One was marked "whites only." That didn't seem right to me, so I went over to the "coloreds only" fountain and sat down. Four waitresses were watching me, but no one came to get my order. I finally got up and went back to the "whites only" fountain. I doubt that I discussed the situation with anyone, but I just knew this wasn't right! Welcome to the world!

Next Daddy pastored the Baptist Church at Davenport, Oklahoma. There I met my best friend, Pauline. I look forward to seeing her in heaven! We were always together.

For my junior high graduation, mother had made me a white dress. She had embroidered colored flowers all around the skirt. Daddy took me to Chandler, a town nearby, so I could pick out my shoes. I was tall, flat-chested and skinny. I chose white platform shoes! Mother and Georgia, my sister, were shocked when they saw them. They couldn't believe that Daddy let me buy them! I just remember him saying, "That's the ones she wanted!"

Another thing I remember that happened there, was one evening after church when we all went outside and looked at what was happening in the sky! It looked like all the stars in the sky were falling. I've never seen anything like it since. I remember hearing someone say, "I think this is a sign that the world is coming to an end."

Recently my daughter researched it for me and found it was called "the meteor shower of October 9, 1946." It was quite a sight!

From Davenport, Daddy pastored a Baptist church at Sand Springs, where I went to high school. His next to the last church in Oklahoma was a country church near Seminole. I didn't want to leave Sand Springs because I was so involved in the speech and drama department. Our coach was Cecil Pickett - who had been the outstanding drama student at the University of Oklahoma. I couldn't bear to leave the competitive program, so I stayed with a friend.

That year at state was one of my most embarrassing moments! I had made it to the finals in extemporaneous speaking. I had read Newsweek and Time magazines all year, so I was ready for any subject! When it was my turn to draw my topic, I drew the subject "Taxi Drivers in New York City."

Each person had to speak at least ten minutes or you were automatically disqualified!

The only thing that I was able to do was talk ten minutes! Worse yet, my speech teacher, Cecil Pickett, was sitting in the back row! I don't remember anything I said, I only knew I talked for ten minutes, or I was in trouble!

Every time I looked at my coach, he was smiling. Sometimes even laughing! It was the longest ten minutes of my life! No, I didn't place! (Maybe last!)

One year when Daddy and Mother were driving to the Baptist convention in Florida, they stopped at a little town called Panacea to go to church. The pastor welcomed them, and when Daddy told them he was a pastor from Oklahoma headed for the Southern Baptist Convention, the pastor asked Daddy if he would like to preach for them! Of course he would - and he did! The little town was southwest of Tallahassee - right on the ocean.

Many years later, when Daddy pastored the Oklahoma Avenue Baptist Church in Shawnee, someone from the Baptist church in Panacea, Florida called Daddy and told him their pastor had retired, and wondered if he might be interested in moving to Panacea as their pastor. Daddy was quick to say 'yes." I was never sure if that was God or the ocean. Daddy loved to fish!

They lived in Panacea for many years until his death following heart surgery.

I honored and respected both my mother and father. But is seems there was little discussion about seeking God's will in our lives or encouraging each other. I'm blaming no one - just trying to figure out how this child lost her way!

7

THE WAY, THE TRUTH AND THE LIFE

Philippians 2:12 TLB

"For God is at work within you, helping you want to <u>obey</u> Him, and <u>then</u> helping you do what He wants."

I've depended upon this beautiful scripture on many occasions - and God has never failed me. In essence Paul is telling us, "God changes your "want to" - And He does!

When Paul was writing to Christians in Corinth (2 Corinthians 6:14,15 NKJ), he gave good advice to them regarding marriage! He said "Do not be unequally yoked together with unbelievers. For what fellowship has righteousness with lawlessness? And what communion has light with darkness?"

I was past fifty years old when I discovered how important discipleship is. There was definitely something important missing in my life - and I was about to find out what it was!

Marriage number five occurred just weeks before I discovered my life-changer! After this marriage, my children were married or in college. We moved to the country.

This was the first time I had ever seen a Christian television program. It was called T.B.N. - The Trinity Broadcasting Network. I was amazed at what I was seeing! I just remember how I felt the presence of God's power that I had never felt before. It wasn't long until I understood that this was the presence of the Holy Spirit! I was still teaching school, but I was watching TBN at every opportunity. I knew one thing - I wanted what they had! I knew, of course, that God was three in one - Father, Son and Holy Spirit. But I didn't know this Person! I learned later, I was what Paul would call a baby Christian!

When I was younger - and went to lots of revivals in those days - we mostly heard sermons on "How to be Saved" - and that is certainly first to be taught - but there is more to follow, and some never find it! Something, I finally learned, called sanctification.

During this same period, my pastor, Robin Cowin, asked me and Vicki Cooper if we would like to be in his discipleship class. We both said "yes!" (We discovered later, we were his class!) This study was called "Masterlife," and it was written by a Baptist missionary, Avery Willis, Jr. I learned so much in this study!

How I wish I could have been discipled right after I got saved! Frankly, I think discipleship should be a prerequisite for church membership! It's never too late, even if you're past fifty! One should not assume a new Christian will grow on his own - even if he attends Sunday school and church.

Masterlife taught me the difference between the natural man, the carnal Christian, and the spiritual Christian!

We know the natural man doesn't know the Lord. The carnal Christian we are going to look at more closely in the next chapter, and the spiritual Christian is our goal!

The spiritual Christian knows what sanctification is! (It's not complicated, as I always thought!) I realize if I had been in the Word, I wouldn't have missed it! I believe we could say that is rule #1 - If we want to grow in our walk with Christ, we must spend time in the Word! We have to make time to put Him first!

I learned the hard way. God will not take second place in anyone's life if one wants to grow, and especially if he wants to be a disciple!

One of our assignments in Masterlife was to start where we were (in our prayer and quiet time) and then add more daily!

Well, I didn't know just how much I prayed daily - probably not much - but I had to start somewhere. So I said ten minutes, and wondered if I could find that much to pray about - and then add more daily! (Buckle your seat belts!)

I can tell you this works, but at the beginning, I wasn't sure! I had many things in my life that were good - and yes, they were first! And I can guarantee you that you will not grow if HE is not first!

I don't care how good or important first is - if it is not God, you will need to regroup! Look at his promise in Matthew (6:32-33 TLB), "...Your heavenly Father knows perfectly well what you need and He will give it to you if you give Him <u>first</u> place in your life and live as He wants you to." And that is a promise! If you give Him second place in your life, you may be saved - but you will not be a disciple! And you will miss out on many blessings!

I learned this from Oswald Chambers, after Vicki gave me his book "My Utmost For His Highest," after completing our Masterlife class. That was thirty or more years ago!

Chambers also said, "There is nothing easier than being saved because it is God's sovereign work. Our Lord never lays down the conditions of discipleship as the conditions for salvation! Discipleship has an option with it." Jesus said in Luke 14:26-27 (NKJ), what it takes to be a disciple. "If anyone comes to Me and does not hate his father and mother, wife and children, brothers and sisters - and yes, even his own life also, he cannot be My disciple, (27) and whoever does not bear his own cross and come after Me, cannot be My disciple."

Now I know that sounds harsh, but "hate" here is a hyperbole which means we must love Jesus more than anyone else! That even includes ourselves! We have to die to self!

It certainly does not happen overnight, it takes years - even a lifetime of devotion to Christ! But dying to self is the most exciting walk there is, and it really is worth the cost!

To press it even more, Jesus said in Luke 14:33 (TLB), "So no one can become My disciple unless he first sits down, and counts his blessings - and then renounce them all for Me." I think of our precious martyrs even today, in so many countries who have paid that price! I'm sure none have regretted it!

Listen to what Jesus said about this situation. He said God already knows your needs and will give them to you. There is just one requirement! Matthew 6:33 (TLB) tells us, "And He will give them to you if you give Him first place in your life and live as He wants you to." In the next chapter, (Matthew 7:13-14 TLB) He reminds us that "Heaven can be entered only through the narrow gate. The highway to hell is broad, and the gate is wide enough for all the multitudes who choose its easy way. (14) But the gateway to life is small, and the road is narrow, and only a few ever find it."

I remember from high school, one of my favorite poems of Robert Frost had a line that expressed the same sentiment. "Two roads diverged into the woods. I took the one less traveled by, and that has made all the difference."

Speaking of putting God first, I was surprised to see this scripture in Deuteronomy giving the same advice! "The purpose of tithing is to teach you always to put God first in your lives." And it does! (Deut. 14:23c TLB)

DISCOVERING THE TRUTH!

Philippians 3:8,13-14 NKJ

"Yet indeed I also count all things loss
<u>for</u> the excellence of the knowledge of
Jesus my Lord, for whom I have suffered
loss of all things, and count them as
<u>rubbish</u> that I might find Christ."

t was in Masterlife that I learned, or at least acknowledged, the difference between the carnal Christian and the spiritual Christian.

Paul called the carnal Christians "babies" and Avery Willis called the baby Christians, carnal. I believe they are one and the same!

We will look closely at what Paul told the baby Christians at Corinth, as well as how Willis described the carnal Christians in the next chapters, but first let's take a look at the natural man.

1Corinthians 2:14 (NKJ) gives us that description: "But the natural man does not receive the things of the Spirit of God for they are foolishness to him! Nor can he know them because they are _spiritually_ discerned." The natural man does not receive the things of the Spirit of God because they are foolish to him - and there is a good reason for this! He doesn't have the Spirit living in him.

Have you ever heard anyone say, "I guess I'm just a nominal Christian?"Nominal means "in name only." One may fool himself because he attended church at one time with other Christians. Or perhaps, says he was "raised in church" because his or her family attended church. If one has not personally accepted Jesus as Lord of his life, he will be one of those standing in line at the "Great White Throne Judgement" who hear these words, "I never knew you,"(Mt 7:23 NKJ). He is also saying, "You never knew Me." Those are not only the saddest words one could ever hear, but terrifying - because then, it will be too late!

Remember when the thief, who was hanging on the

crosse next to Jesus, realized that Jesus was indeed the Messiah. The thief asked Jesus to remember him <u>when</u> He came into His kingdom. Jesus - <u>knowing his heart</u> - told him then, "Today you will be with me in paradise!"(Luke 23:40-43 TLB)

This scripture says it all! The Father who sent Jesus is in charge. <u>He draws people to</u> <u>Me</u> - That's the only way you'll ever come to Me. Only then do I do my work, putting people together, setting them on their feet, ready for the end. (*paraphrase* John 5:37;6:65 TLB)

This is one important reason <u>we must</u> <u>pray for the lost ones</u> around us - family and friends! Because it is our prayers that can awaken these lost ones to understand <u>their need to know the truth.</u> *Then* the Father draws him! John 6:44 (NIV) tells us that! For no one can come to me <u>unless</u> the Father who sent Me draws him to me…" Wow!

THE BABY CHRISTIANS AT CORINTH

1st Corinthians 2:9 9 (TLB)

"But it is written: Eye has not seen, nor ear heard, nor have entered into the heart of man the things which God has prepared for those who love Him."

I n 1Corinthians 3 (TLB), Paul makes it clear that he knows about the divisions in the church, and said there is just on reason! You are all babies! "Dear brothers, I have been talking to you as though you are still babies in the Christian life, who are not following the Lord, but your own desires! I cannot talk to you as I would healthy Christians who are _filled_ with the Spirit. I have had to feed you with milk, not solid food, because you couldn't digest anything stronger. And even now you still have to be on milk. For you are still only baby Christians controlled by your own desires, not God's." (1 Corinthians 3:1-3a TLB)

This letter from Paul helped me to understand that, yes - I was a Christian, but just a baby. I was an adult who hadn't grown because I had failed to put Christ first in my life! And being a baby Christian, I missed the most important piece of advice I desperately needed. As mentioned earlier, the Corinthian Church was weak and the city was wicked.

So here Paul is again, reminding them of something they needed to remember, "Don't be teamed with those who do not love the Lord, for what do people of God have in common with the people of sin? How can light live with darkness And what harmony can be between Christ and the devil? How can a Christian be a partner with one who doesn't believe?" (2 Corinthians 6:14,15 TLB)

Probably the greatest danger of all, is staying a baby Christian! We miss out on so much joy when our eyes are on ourselves - and not the purpose He has for our lives!

Lastly, make certain you really do know the Lord! The greatest problem of every person is this: Because Adam and

Eve's great sin in the Garden of Eden - we were all born sinners in need of a Savior. Having a church membership or growing up in church is not a basis of salvation for anyone. And going to heaven is much more than getting a passport stamped! True salvation is not just knowing who Jesus is, but actually _knowing_ Him in a personal relationship!

Double check 1 Corinthians 15:1-2 (TLB)!

Paul is speaking, "Now let me remind you, brothers, of what the Gospel really is, for it has not changed - it is the same good news I preached to you before.

You welcomed it then and still do now, for your faith is squarely built upon this wonderful message; (2) and it is this Good news that saves you if you still firmly believe it, unless of course, you never really believed it in the first place!"

None of us are perfect yet, but like Paul, we can daily crucify the flesh, ask for God's forgiveness - and He will forgive!

We grow stronger with each year of study and prayer! But we must get in the word. We must know each member of the Trinity! Yes - they are one, but if you neglect one person, you can still be ignorant of who God is - who Jesus is - or who the Holy Spirit is!

In my life, what was first was not necessarily bad. It was just that it was in the wrong place. I remember when someone from another town called and asked me to direct their dinner theater - I quickly said, "no, I couldn't," with little explanation, because I hardly understood it myself. I just knew what used to be first in my life was no longer first! I finally understood that the only place He will take, if you want to be a disciple, is first! And I wanted to be His disciple!

If we don't want a battle going on in our life - conflicting influences that are fighting one another, there really is an easy solution.

We simply do what Paul said in Galatians 5:24 (TLB) tells us to do! "Those who belong to Christ have nailed their natural desires to His cross and crucified them there."

Paul goes on in his letter to the Galatians in the next two verses. (Gal 5:25, 26 TLB) "If we are living now by the Holy Spirit, let us follow the Holy Spirit's leading in every part of our lives. Then we don't need to look for honors and popularity, which lead to jealousy and hard feelings."

I remember how I needed to look for honors and popularity to prove I was ok!

THE CARNAL CHRISTIAN

1 Corinthians 3:11-15 NKJ

"For no other foundation can anyone lay than that which is laid, which is Jesus Christ.

(12) Now if anyone builds on this foundation with gold, silver, precious stones, wood, hay, straw, (13) each one's work will become clear, for the Day will declare it, because it will be revealed by fire; and the fire will test each one's work, of what sort it is. (14) If anyone's work which he has built on endures, he will receive a reward. (15) If anyone's work is burned, he will suffer loss, but he himself will be saved, yet as through fire."

t is my hope that others will be helped as much by Avery Willis Jr's description of the carnal Christian, as I was. This was a different description than Paul gave us in 1st Corinthians, but later we see they are both talking about the carnal (baby) Christian!

I can't explain how much this made sense to me! I've always tried to understand why I always had such low self-image. My first perception of my lack of self-esteem came from the stories I've shared of my being molested when I was a little girl. Those pictures have never left my mind. I'm fairly certain they helped shape my perception of who I was, but Willis' description of the carnal Christian gave me hope!

Willis says that at sometime in his life, the carnal Christian has opened the door of the Spirit, but left open the door of the flesh!! He was talking about me! I was a carnal Christian! I had opened my heart to Jesus - I knew that - but I had left open the door to the flesh! And there was certainly a battle going on in my life! I had never understood how I could continue to make the same mistakes over and over! Here was my answer! Yes, I had opened the door to Jesus, to the Spirit, to Father God - but I had left open the door to the flesh! I think that door was open for years! I have such a deep gratitude for TBN, and the truth they shared about the Holy Spirit! Trinity Broadcasting Network, 38 years ago, certainly helped me understand the third person in the Trinity! And I am forever grateful - as there was a battle going on in my life! And as long as the door of my heart was still open to the flesh, I was on my own! And trying to battle the flesh and its desires is not a good place to be. I was living proof!

Jesus said to his disciples in Matthew 26:41b (NKJ), "... the spirit is willing, but the flesh is weak." It takes the power of the Holy Spirit to overcome our weak flesh to keep in step with God's perfect will for our lives.

The enemy still has easy access to our thoughts, our will and our emotions! This is so important. If we do not put Christ first in our life, we are going to have difficulties. I can't repeat it often enough. We have to first close the door to the flesh, and put God first!

I remember when I first learned this, I was busy with our own dinner theater in Okeene, school plays, competitive speech contests - the things that were first in my life - many, like the dinner theater had nothing to do with my school work - I also loved movies, the theater - lots of things, but they all were what I loved doing. And I loved doing them more than I loved God! He was not even close to first place in my life!

During this time a friend in another town called and asked me to direct their dinner theater production! I had to say "no," hardly understanding myself. I just knew I had to change who and what was first in my life! I had a new goal, a new passion! Becoming a disciple!

At some point in his life the carnal Christian has realized that Jesus could give him eternal life - he opened the door of the Spirit and was born again. But he failed to grow as he should. His mistake was that he left open the door of the flesh! When that happens, we know who now has access to our thoughts, our will, and our emotions!

The conflict in our life, or personality, is because we

hear the voice of Satan through our flesh - we have become a battleground!

I loved Willis' description of the carnal Christian because it seemed what happened in my own life.

And there certainly is a solution! "Those who belong to Christ have nailed their natural desires to His cross and crucified them there. If we are living now by the Holy Spirit's power, let us follow the Holy Spirit's leading in every part of our lives. Then we won't have to look for honors and popularity, which lead to jealousy and hard feelings." (Gal 5:24-26 TLB)

Anyone of us should ask ourselves these questions:

(1) Am I a natural man who does not have Jesus in my life? Am I being controlled by my natural desires?

(2) Am I a Carnal Christian who has asked Jesus to come into my life, but has left open the door to the flesh? And if so, is there a battle going on?

Paul, when he was a natural man and didn't know Jesus, was going about his daily activities of causing persecution and the killing of many Christians when God stopped him on the road to Damascus and asked him, "Saul, Saul, why are you persecuting me?" (Acts 9:4 TLB)

God changed his life so dramatically, that Paul wrote most of the New Testament! If He could do that for Paul, he certainly can do that for anyone who wants change. (No matter our past!) If one realizes he is a carnal Christian, there is certainly hope! Paul encourages us in Galatians 5:16

(TLB) "I advise you to obey the Holy Spirit's instructions. He will tell you where to go and what to do, and then you won't always be doing the wrong things your evil nature wants you to do." Shut the door! - And the Holy Spirit will let you know if that door has been left open - oh, yes!

We know that we are not perfect yet, but we also know that when we are tempted, we have a Father who loves us and is ready to help us be an overcomer! I know there would never have been a fifth (or second) marriage in my life if I had known how to be a spiritual Christian. I did my best to live peacefully with the man I married the last time, again, for all the wrong reasons - until he passed, at the age of 94 after 35 years of a very difficult marriage. He was a good man in many ways - many people loved him. But to me, he was always verbally abusive. I cannot mention the many derogatory names he has called me over the years - always leaving me in tears. The outbursts were always over nothing!

I'm not sure which hurts the most, physical abuse or verbal abuse. I've had both, but I sometimes think hateful words hurt the most. My daughter was a nurse at the Veteran's Hospital for many years. She told me he definitely exhibited signs of PTSD and we should get him tested. She worked with many service men who suffered mentally from war trauma. She was probably right. He was on his ship during WW II, when it was torpedoed, and many of his buddies were killed. He helped remove the bodies from the ship.

I probably should have listened to her, but he never thought he had a problem, and I didn't want to give him a reason to get upset. But her diagnosis helped me remember there might have been a good reason for his hateful outbursts. In any case, I just kept asking God to give me patience! One thing that helped endure (especially towards the end of his life) was reminding myself (this was from God!) Jesus was spit upon, and called awful names. Acts 8:32b (TLB) says, "He opened not his mouth."

God gave me the grace to endure throughout my last marriage. It was difficult, but having the power of the Holy Spirit was not only a comfort for me, but He helped me overcome in the face of incredible difficulty! If I hadn't opened the door for the Holy Spirit in my life, the outcome would have definitely been much different - without a doubt! By the grace of God, I was able to love him and take care of him until the very end.

THE DANGER OF BEING
A BABY CHRISTIAN

John 15:5 NKJ

"I am the vine, you are the branches. He who abides in me, and I in him, bears much fruit; for without Me you can do <u>nothing</u>!"

Yes, there are dangers in being a baby Christian. First of all, for anyone who was a slow learner, like I was, there is so much I regret in having wasted so many years!

Secondly, if you raised children, you realize you have not given them a firm foundation on which to build their lives. Yes, I took them to church, they were in Sunday school and Bible school - but there were no family devotions, reading Bible stories together and experiencing the blessings of praying together. There is a greater danger, of course. If you haven't been discipled, and have never grown in your walk with Christ, you can easily be used by the enemy to keep you a baby. And I might emphasize, that you do not live unto yourself. Your life has an impact on every person you interact with - and in the big scheme of life, this impact can be eternal, good or bad.

There is an old saying, that is so true, "one I love, and one I hate, but the one I feed will dominate!" Have you ever been to a nature refuge and seen the sign, "Do not feed the animals?" Because what you feed demands more. When we feed our flesh, it demands more. And that shuts the door on the voice of the Holy Spirit in our life and His guidance. And we _need_ to be able to hear the voice of the Holy Spirit!

Of course this means you could turn your back on God and join the crowd. But you will have no joy, no blessings, and no rewards in heaven. The problem with compromise in a Christian's life is this: You have enough of God in your life, you can't enjoy walking in sin. And you have enough compromise/sin in your life, it's hard to enjoy a relationship with God. I've always felt if anyone really denied Jesus, after being saved and knowing His love, how could he deny Him? My experience when I was seven, made me think I was a Christian. I had been baptized and was a member of the church! Thank God for the Holy Spirit! He is the one who directed that lady behind me at youth camp! Though I didn't know who it was at the time, the Holy Spirit (through her) certainly let me know I needed Jesus. When I was twelve, I knew I had made a mistake following my sister down the aisle. I knew I wasn't a Christian, and if I died, I wouldn't have gone to heaven!

I lived with that fear for four or five years. Because I was a member of the church and my daddy was the pastor! I didn't share the fear with anyone - not even my parents! I remember reading somewhere, that Jesus would rather have one sold-out disciple than 100 church members who are carnal Christians. I think that's a true statement!

I discovered a book a year or two ago that opened my eyes to something I had missed in my "growing up in Christ" years. The book was "Driven by Eternity," by John Bevere, published by Messenger International 2017. I began to understand the impact of the following scriptures in light of eternity.

For those who have never read these scriptures, it might encourage you to get serious - if you need a "push!" The truth is that, as Believers, we will all have to stand before God and be judged! This includes our sins we commit, and those of omission. For example, if we have been given the opportunity to witness to someone, and we fail to be obedient, that is listed!! Let's look at 2 Corinthians 5:10 (TLB), "For we all must stand before Christ to be judged and have our lives laid bare before Him. Each of us will receive whatever he deserves for the good or bad things he has done in his earthly body." In 1 Corinthians 3:12-15 (TLB), Paul talks about a Christian's works in the body being tested by fire. If it was sinful, compromise, or dead works - those done out of duty for Christ and not done out of love for Christ - Paul says they will be burned up. And we will suffer loss. When I think of the price Jesus paid for my life, He took my wrath, and I should be in hell… I have already suffered loss from the years I did not live for Christ and again for the years when He was not first in my life. The last thing I want is to stand before Him on that day and have nothing to offer. My best explanation of the judgement seat of Christ, with Jesus evaluating our life is this: *His rewards are His way of showing you **how He feels about the way you loved Him** in this life*!   I want my works to survive the testing of the fire of God! Don't you? Yes, we are standing in line with all of His children, but our rewards will depend on that judgement Paul talks about. If that isn't a "wake up call," I don't know what is. Yes, we will be in heaven, but we will also face the judgement seat of Christ! And on that day, I do not want any regrets!

Now, "the Great White Throne judgement" mentioned in Revelation 20:12 (NKJ), is for those who have never accepted Jesus as Lord. I believe many will not only be shocked, but terrified when they hear these words from Jesus, *"…**I never knew you; Depart from Me you who practice lawlessness!"*** (Matthew 7:22-23 NKJ) We should all have a prayer list with names of family, friends or co-workers who do not know what awaits them!

12

TIME TO GROW UP KNOW THE HOLY SPIRIT!

John 16:13 NKJ

"...when He, the Spirit of Truth has come, He will guide you unto all Truth: for He will speak on His own authority, but whatever He hears He will speak, and He will tell you things to come."

AMEN!

As you know, this was for me the most neglected Person of the Trinity. When I say "neglected," I mean many of us failed to understand the person of the Holy Spirit for lack of teaching in the church we attended!

When I was young, I think many of the churches in my denomination didn't want to appear "Pentecostal," so they pretty much ignored His place in the Trinity! That might sound harsh, but that is the only explanation I could come up with! I know times have changed over the years and the person and work of the Holy Spirit is being more and more acknowledged.

Jesus told His disciples, "Anyone who doesn't obey me, doesn't love me. I'm telling you these things now, while I am still with you. But when the Father sends the Comforter, instead of me - and by the Comforter, I mean the Holy Spirit - He will teach you much, as well as remind you of everything I myself have told you." (John 14:24-26 TLB)

I know most of us have been told that we are sealed with the Holy Spirit when we become Christians - and we are, but 2 Corinthians 1:22 (TLB) tells us more! The Apostle Paul writes that "He has put His brand upon us" - His mark of ownership - and given us the Holy Spirit in our heart as a <u>guarantee that we belong to Him, and as the first installment of all He is going to give us!</u> (A first installment is a guarantee - or a promise that more is coming!)

I remember when several women from our prayer group went to Oklahoma City to hear Marilyn Hickey speak (we had seen her on T.V.) I don't recall the place where it was held, but it was filled to capacity. After her teaching she invited anyone who wanted the baptism of the Holy Spirit to go to the room behind the stage. Of course everyone there knew I was ready to go! We had all noticed a couple from Okeene (not from our church) and some, I think, were reluctant to let them know that some of "us Baptists" were interested! I said, "Let's go!" - but I was outvoted - and so we left and went to Shepherd's Mall instead! It was the largest mall in Oklahoma City at that time! Anyway, I wanted so badly to go with the group "behind the stage," but since we were all in the same car, I thought it best to go to the mall.

As we parked our car, and walked to towards the mall, I could feel something stirring inside of me - I really couldn't describe it, but when we got to the door, I was pretty sure what was happening! God knew my heart and how much I wanted to be filled - baptized - with the Holy Spirit.

When the girls opened the door, I left the group and said, "I'll catch up with you later, I want to check this store," and turned the other direction. The movement that had begun in my midsection was moving to my mouth! I wonder if I had known what to do next, I would be speaking in tongues - but I didn't know! I just knew God knew my heart and baptized me with His Holy Spirit, and I would never be the same!

Many people do not understand there are three baptisms! If you have not read Robert Morris' book, "The God I Never Knew," you may not understand this statement. His book is a classic, as far as I'm concerned. If you are wondering about the Baptism of the Holy Spirit, I highly recommend it!

Let's review quickly the three baptisms. The first baptism we are going to talk about is found in 1Cor 12:13b (TLB), "But the Holy Spirit has fitted us all together into one body. We have been baptized into Christ's body by one Spirit, and have all been given that same Holy Spirit." Notice the Holy Spirit is the one who baptized us into the body of Christ, the Church. Notice the prepositions, telling us who is doing the action. "For by one Spirit we were all baptized into one body."

Then if you are obedient to the command of the scripture, we choose to experience a second baptism. This one is immersion in water. It is an outward sign of what has happened inwardly. John said, "I baptize you with water, but the One more powerful than I will come, the thongs of whose sandals I am not worthy to untie. He will baptize you with the Holy Spirit and fire!" (Matthew 3:11 NKJ)

In his book, "The God I Never Knew," Robert Morris paraphrases John's statement like this. "You've seen me immersing repentant people in water, but I am just a forerunner for a much greater one, Jesus, who will immerse reborn people in the fire of the Holy Spirit."

Morris also points out in his book, something I had never noticed before. He says pay attention to the prepositions, because they tell you who is doing the action - or the baptizing! (This is what prepositions do!) This really spoke to my heart! Being an English teacher for many years, surprisingly, I had neglected to notice what was obvious in the scriptures! I was always taught that we were sealed with the Holy Spirit - and we were! Look at 2 Cor 1:22 (TLB). "He has put His brand upon us - His mark of ownership - and given us His Holy Spirit in our hearts <u>as a guarantee</u>

that we belong to Him, and as the <u>first installment</u> of all He is going to give us." What then is a first installment? That means more is coming! All we have to do is ask! See also Acts 2:33 (TLB), which talks about the promised Holy Spirit being poured out on Believers; and also John 1:33 (TLB) - John the Baptist states he will baptize with water, but Jesus is the one who will baptize with the Holy Spirit!

SANCTIFICATION

2 Corinthians 3:18 NKJ

"But we all, with unveiled face, beholding as in a mirror the glory of the Lord, are being transformed into the same image from glory to glory just as by the spirit of the Lord."

Make time daily to get into the Word of God. That is number one! I began early in the morning because I was working. It just seemed right for me to start my day with prayer and reading the Word.

Jesus always made time to get off by Himself and pray! His disciples noticed this, of course, and finally asked Him to teach them to pray - and He did! Isn't it interesting that the disciples were with Jesus 24 hours a day/seven days a week for over three years, and the only thing they asked Jesus to teach them was about prayer!

There are so many good teaching books and devotionals that I still read daily during my quiet time. The first is Oswald Chambers, "My Utmost For His Highest," which was first published and copyrighted by Discovery House in 1935. I was impressed by the introduction which was written by the Chaplain of the United States Senate. He said, No book, except the Bible, has influenced my walk with Christ at such deep and maturing levels." I agree with this statement! I claim Oswald Chambers as my mentor. I've read his devotional daily since it was given to me over thirty years ago. It seems I learn something new everyday! I did eventually purchase the "updated" version for several reasons. Sometimes I run across an "old English" word and I wanted to compare it to the new edition! My friend Vicki was the one who gave me this book!

Another book which has taught me so much about prayer is another "oldie," written by Andrew Murray. It was given to me by a member of my Sunday school class, (Donna B.). It had belonged to her dad who was a Baptist preacher. The title is "With Christ in the School of Prayer," (published by Whitaker House in 1984). She gave it to me five or six years ago, and I just keep reading it, a little every morning. My grandson gave me a big thick book for Christmas this past year, that has a collection of Murray's seven books on prayer! So I know that's available! (I plan to start reading it after I completely finish writing this book!)

Murray describes the person of God in this way. "You are the Father, infinite in Your love and power. As the Son, You are my redeemer and my life. And as the Holy Spirit, You are my strength." What a mighty God we serve!

I want to mention a book written by Warren and Ruth Myers, which was popular in the nineties, but is just as powerful today. It's called "31 Days of Praise," (published in 1994) A reminder to praise God daily! I know God wants to hear His children praising and thanking Him! The margins in this book are full of things that happened on that date. Sometimes I forgot to put the year, much to my regret! But I am so thankful for my friend, Leslie, who gave this book to me!

I love the little book, "Jesus Calling," written by Sarah Young and published by Thomas Nelson in 2004. It's just a sweet reminder that Jesus is watching over me and that He loves me. This is an excellent book to give to a new Christian, and even to one who is going through a hard time!

The key word to growth, I believe, is obedience. Jesus told His disciples, "The one who loves me, my Father will love him, and I will too, and I will reveal myself to him." (*paraphrase* John 14:21 TLB). And He will!

There is a quote by Vance Havener I love, "Jesus Christ

is the first and last, author and finisher, beginning and end, alpha and omega, and by Him all other things hold together. He must be first or nothing. God never comes next!" As long as the beauty of God fascinates our heart, He will always win first place in our hearts - He will never be an afterthought. There is none like Him! However, cultivating a fascination with Him takes time and must be a priority in our schedules! Once you experience how beautiful our Heavenly Father is, growing up will be a product of the process. And before you know it, the Holy Spirit will be leading you every step of the way until you finally see Him face to face and place your hand in His. I can't fathom what it will be like to touch the holes where the stakes held our Messiah to the cross! What a glorious day that will be!

14

GROWING UP TAKES A LIFETIME

Matthew 6:6 NKJ

"But you, when you pray, go into your room, and when you have shut your door, pray to your Father who is in the secret place; and your Father who sees in secret will reward you openly."

In conclusion, I feel there is one important point that needs to be stressed if one truly wants to "grow up." I can promise you that it is not only necessary, but if you choose to try without it, you will be disappointed!

We each need a private place where we can be alone with the Father, with His word, our prayer lists and requests!

God has promised us that He will not abandon what He has begun! "And I am sure that God who began the good work in you will keep right on helping you grow in His grace until his task within you is finally finished on that day when Jesus Christ returns."(Philippians 1:6 TLB)

The altar is where we go to meet the one who can alter our old habits. I promise you, that if you are faithfully spending your quiet time with Him, one day you will be able to say, "This is the best part of my day!"

Jesus reminded His disciples to wait in Jerusalem until they received the Comforter - the Holy Spirit. He also said, "But the fact of the matter is that it is best for you that I go away, for if I don't, the Comforter will not come. If I do, He will - for I will send Him to you." (John 16:7 TLB)

Luke added his thoughts as well, saying "and if sinful persons like yourselves give children what they need, don't you realize that your heavenly Father will do at least as much, and give the Holy Spirit to those who ask for Him?" (Luke 11:13 TLB)

Paul adds that, "He has put His brand upon us - his mark of ownership - and given us His Holy Spirit in our hearts as guarantee that we belong to Him, *and as the first installment of all that He is going to give us!"* (2 Corinthians 1:22 TLB)

The last thing He shouted to His disciples before He left them was "Tarry in city of Jerusalem until you are endued with power from on high!" (Luke 24:49b NKJ)

And lastly, this verse has served me well over the years, as I have relied on it daily… "(15) If you love me, keep my commandments. (16) And I will pray to the Father and He will give you another Helper, that He will abide with you forever- (17) the Spirit of truth, whom the world cannot receive, because it neither sees Him nor knows Him; but you know Him for He dwells with you <u>and will be in you</u>. (18) I will not leave you orphans; I will come to you." (John 14:15-18 NKJ). And John 14:7 Jesus makes this promise to His disciples, "…it is best if I go away, because if I don't, the Advocate won't come. If I do go away, then I will send Him to you."

My final thought is this: don't ever leave home without the Holy Spirit. Unbroken communion with Him each and every day is essential for every believer whether you have just been born again, or you have been walking with the Lord for 40 plus years! And that is the secret of growing up in the Lord!

If you have read this book and realize you have never accepted Jesus as your Savior, it's not too late! Just as the thief on the cross cried out to Jesus, "Remember, me when you come into your Kingdom!" (Luke 23:42 TLB) God will hear you when you ask Him to accept you as His child and He will guide you and grow you daily! Yes, He died for you… there is no greater love!